Green Cuisine™
with
Glenda Gourley

Green Cuisine

Glenda Gourley

REED

Published by Reed Books, a division of Reed Publishing (NZ) Ltd,
39 Rawene Rd, Birkenhead, Auckland.
www.reed.co.nz.
Associated companies,
branches and representatives throughout the world.

ISBN 0 7900 0683 9

Cover and text designed by Sunny H. Yang
Photography by Alan Gillard
Food Assistant, Anne Gourley

First published 1999

Printed in New Zealand

contents

Introduction

Green Cuisine screens weekly on TV3 with easy, tasty and healthy vegetable ideas. This recipe book is a collection of some of those wonderful recipes and tips.

Green Cuisine is the campaign of the New Zealand Vegetable & Potato Growers' Federation Inc. This organisation, known in the industry as Vegfed, accepts a responsibility to promote the health value of vegetables and represents approximately 3500 commercial growers from throughout the country.

Growers make the greatest possible efforts to ensure the quality and freshness of their vegetables. We trust that these recipes will increase your enjoyment of our fantastic produce!

Veg ed

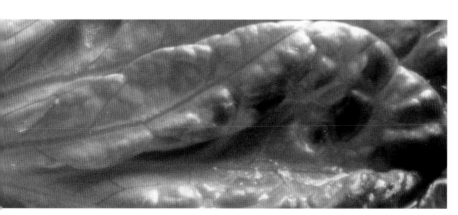

New Zealand Vegetable & Potato Growers' Federation Inc.
PO Box 10-232
Wellington
Ph: 04 472 3795
Fax: 04 471 2861
For more information visit our website
www.greencuisine.co.nz

Why are vegetables so perishable?

After harvesting, vegetables are still alive. To preserve freshness, the best you can do is to slow down the rate at which they die — you can't stop it completely. The following are some tips that will help you get the most from the vegetables you purchase.

- To stay fresh, vegetables need oxygen so that they can continue to 'breathe', or respire. Different vegetables breathe at different rates. This is why some vegetables last longer than others. *Respiration is slowed by refrigeration.*

- Vegetables are covered with micro-organisms, which cause decay given the right conditions of warmth and humidity. Bruises and cuts allow the entrance of these organisms and speed up decay. *Refrigeration is the best method of reducing decay* as most micro-organisms slow right down at low temperatures.

- *Refrigeration also retards deterioration caused by chemical and biological reactions.* For example, sweetcorn may lose 50% of its initial sugar content in a single day at 21°C, while only 5% will be lost in one day at 0°C.

- *Many colour changes associated with aging and ripening can also be delayed and slowed by refrigeration.*

- Loss of moisture, with consequent wilting and shrivelling, is one of the obvious ways in which freshness is lost. *Most vegetables are best kept in a humid place – your vegetable crisper or a plastic bag is fine.*

- The effect of rough handling is cumulative. Bruising increases the rate of respiration and hence shortens life. Damage also results in more moisture loss and flavour changes. *Take care never to squash or drop your vegetables.*

- A lot of fruits, like apples, tomatoes, stone fruit, bananas, avocados, kiwifruit, pears and melons, release a gas called ethylene. So does produce which is damaged or bruised. Vegetables like green leafy vegetables, broccoli, carrot, cauliflower, courgette, cucumber and eggplant decay faster when exposed to ethylene. *If you can, separate these foods – keep fruit in a fruit bowl and vegetables in the fridge.*

Tips for buying and storing vegetables ...

Start with quality. You can't produce a wonderful vegetable dish if you don't start with good-quality vegetables!

Buy regularly. Every few days if possible: it is better to buy smaller quantities more often. *There is no doubt, fresher tastes better!*

Store vegetables correctly. Storage greatly affects shelf life. Store your fruit and vegetables correctly as soon as possible after purchasing. Each hour sitting on a bench or in the car decreases their lifespan.

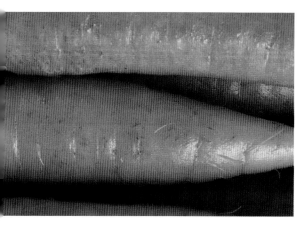

- Keep potatoes, onions, garlic and kumara in a cool dark place. A cardboard box is perfect. *These vegetables do not benefit from refrigeration!*

- Put tomatoes with the ethylene-producing fruit in your fruit bowl.

- *Everything else should go in the fridge.*

How many vegetables should I eat?

To stay healthy you need to eat five or more servings of fresh fruit and vegetables every day. Specifically, three or more servings of vegetables and two or more servings of fruit. All health professionals agree on the recommendation of five or more servings per day.

An easy way to remember this is by looking at your hand. Each finger represents at least one serving of fresh fruit or vegetables. You can easily measure your serving size by imagining what you can fit into the palm of your hand. Therefore an adult's serving is much larger than a child's.

One serving can be a combination of fruit and vegetables (e.g. salads or stir-fries) or a single fruit or vegetable (e.g. a baked potato, an apple or a handful of sliced carrots).

Fresh vegetables make a healthy food choice by supplying a wide range of nutrients including vitamins, minerals and fibre, which help keep us healthy. In addition, many of these components are thought to play a protective role against lifestyle diseases such as cancers and heart disease.

The anti-cancer link

The foods we eat can influence the risk of getting many types of cancer. Experts estimate that 10-70% of cancers are affected by what we eat and drink. More than 150 studies show that people who eat lots of fresh vegetables have the best protection against cancers.

At least 600 phytochemicals (plant chemicals including antioxidants) in vegetables are biologically active and may have a role in cancer prevention. Vitamin pills contain only 3-5 of these phytochemicals so supplement users are shortchanging themselves. Taking one vitamin or mineral is not enough — we need to digest these substances together. We don't know which phytochemicals are important or what the reaction is between them, but we do know that vegetables provide a delicious cocktail which is certainly beneficial to our health.

Fibre helps maintain a healthy digestive system. It produces compounds which protect against some cancers and may also help residues move through the bowel faster, diluting cancer-causing substances and allowing less time to do damage.

Preventing heart disease

Eating foods which are low in fat, salt and sugar and high in fibre is thought to significantly reduce the risk of heart disease. Vegetables are naturally low in fat, salt and sugar and high in fibre. They contain literally hundreds of substances known as antioxidants. These help prevent cholesterol from clogging arteries and are able to decrease the risk of heart disease.

Maintaining a healthy body weight

Because vegetables are naturally low in fat they make a wonderful choice for those wanting to maintain a healthy body weight and avoid obesity.

It is important to select cooking methods and recipes, like most of the ones in this book, which do not add a lot of fat, salt or sugar and which retain as much fibre as possible.

5+a DAY

at 5 or more servings of fresh fruit & vegetables everyday for better health, taste and variety.

Which potato should I use?

Different varieties of potato vary tremendously when they are cooked. For best results, you should choose the variety suited to your needs.

What is a waxy potato?

A waxy potato has a waxy texture. Early-season potatoes are waxy because their sugar has not yet converted to starch; this happens with age. Waxy potatoes tend to be best for boiling, salads and adding to casseroles and soups. They tend to hold their shape and won't fall apart. Because waxy potatoes have a higher sugar content they are not suitable for chipping, roasting or wedges as the sugar will burn. They are also unsuitable for mashing as they go gluey.

What is an all-purpose potato?

There are some varieties which fall into an 'all-purpose' category. These can be cooked using any method, perhaps with not as good results as the ones which clearly fall into the floury or waxy category.

What is a floury potato?

A floury potato has a floury texture. It is low in moisture and sugar, and high in starch. Floury potatoes tend to be best for mashing and baking. They will also make golden chips, roast potatoes or wedges. They tend not to hold their shape so are usually best not used for salads.

However...

As the season progresses the composition of a potato changes. For example, an Ilam Hardy early in the season (October) is quite waxy. As it gets older it is a good all-purpose potato, while towards the end of the season, when a lot more of the natural sugars have converted to starch, it becomes quite floury! Not all potatoes show such a range of characteristics.

Weather, climate and soil also have an effect on the cooking performance of a potato. For example, a Southland-grown Nadine may be very waxy while a Pukekohe-grown Nadine may be only slightly waxy. Flavour is also influenced by these conditions.

If you don't know what sort of potatoes you have bought...

The first time you cook potatoes from a new bag be prepared to adapt your intended serving method once they are cooked and you can tell if they are waxy or floury. For example, if you have boiled a potful intending to mash them, but they have held their shape well and are obviously waxy, don't mash them; toss in a little fresh mint and butter and serve them whole instead. Thereafter, you will know how that bag of potatoes will perform.

Potatoes which tend to be waxy are...
- *most early-season (new) potatoes*
- *Nadine*
- *Draga*
- *Jersey Bennie*
- *Frisia*

All-purpose potatoes are ...
- *Rua*
- *Desiree*
- *Karaka*
- *Rocket*
- *Stroma*

Potatoes which tend to be floury are ...
- *Ilam Hardy*
- *Russet Burbank*
- *Red Rascal*
- *Agria*
- *Fiana*
- *White Delight*

Waxy potatoes are ideal for ...
Boiling
Salads
Casseroles
Soups

All-purpose are suitable for most uses.

Floury potatoes are ideal for ...
Mashing
Baking
Roasting
Chips
Wedges

If in doubt, ask your retailer if a potato is likely to be floury or waxy.

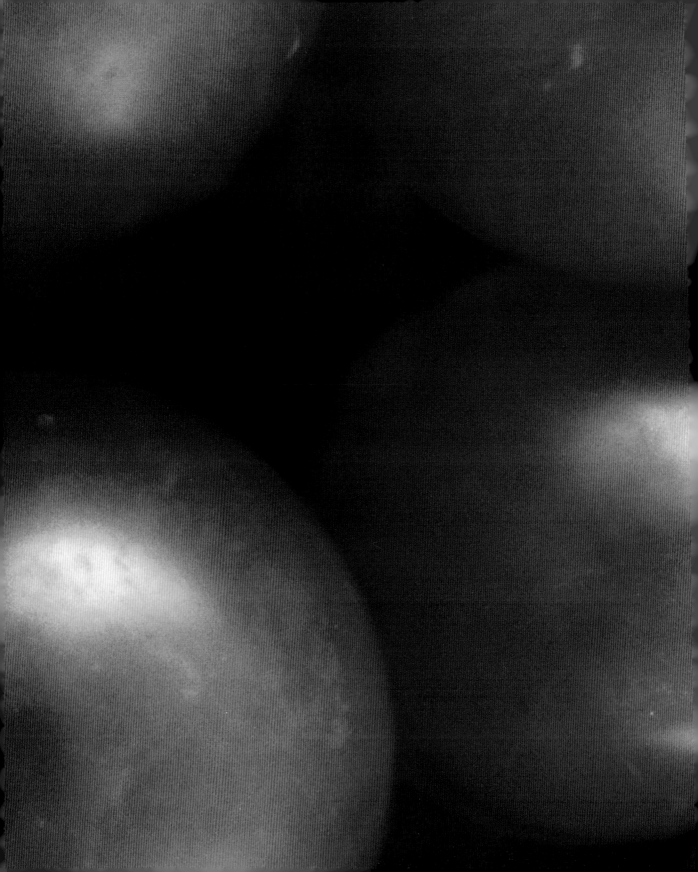

Meals

12-15 mesclun mix/lettuce leaves
1^1/$_2$ cups tomato wedges
2 peppers, sliced
2 cups lightly blanched broccoli florets
3 cups cooked, chunky-sliced golden kumara
100 g thinly sliced pastrami
   OR 350 g beef sirloin or scotch fillet,
   rare roasted and sliced thinly
^{1}/$_2$ small prince or honeydew melon, peeled,
   de-seeded and sliced

Beef and Horseradish Salad

A wonderful combination of flavours makes this colourful salad meal a favourite.

Arrange the salad greens on individual serving plates. Arrange/scatter the tomatoes, peppers, broccoli, kumara, beef and melon slices over the lettuce. Blend the sour cream, horseradish sauce and milk until smooth and creamy, adding a little extra milk if necessary to achieve a pouring consistency. Drizzle over the salad. Serves 4.

Dressing

^{1}/$_2$ cup sour cream or plain yoghurt
1 Tbsp horseradish cream sauce
2 Tbsp milk

To blanch vegetables, place in a saucepan of boiling water for a couple of minutes and then cool under cold running water. They'll still be a bit crunchy and a vibrant colour.

4 rashers (200 g) bacon
2 pita breads
1 bunch well-washed spinach
  (discard outer leaves and stalks)
  OR 12-15 assorted lettuce leaves
2 red-skinned apples, cut into wedges
3 sticks celery, sliced
2 cups cherry tomatoes
  OR 5 tomatoes, cut into slices
4 eggs, lightly poached

Bacon and Egg Salad

This salad meal is especially popular with men.

Remove rind and visible fat from the bacon. Cut into 2 cm squares. Lightly fry in a non-stick fry pan or microwave on high power for 2-3 minutes or until cooked. Split the pita breads, toast, and cut into triangles/wedges. Arrange the spinach leaves on four plates and add the apples, celery and tomatoes. Add the bacon and pita bread. Top with the eggs. Blend dressing ingredients together and pour over salad. Serve immediately.
Serves 4.

Dressing

2 Tbsp oil
¼ cup lemon juice or vinegar
1 tsp poppy seeds
1 Tbsp sugar
freshly ground black pepper

8-10 lettuce leaves (iceberg)
2 cups watercress sprigs
1 cup crunchy bean sprouts
3 spring onions, sliced
2 cups chopped or sliced cucumber
2 cups prepared fruit, e.g. halved
   strawberries, chunks of melon,
   pawpaw or persimmon, kiwifruit
1 cup sliced smoked chicken
2 cups crispy noodles

Fresh and absolutely delicious!

Arrange the lettuce and watercress on serving plates. Top with the sprouts, spring onions, cucumber, fruit, chicken and noodles. Blend the lemon juice, oil and sugar together until the sugar dissolves and pour over salad.
Serves 4.

Fruity Watercress and Chicken Salad

If your lettuce, or any other leafy vegetable or herb, isn't as crisp as you want it, soak it in warm water for a couple of minutes, then refrigerate in a plastic bag or covered container for twenty minutes — it'll be just like new!

Dressing

¼ cup lemon or lime juice
¼ cup light olive oil
2 Tbsp sugar
freshly ground black pepper

Warm Creamy Chicken Salad

4-6 waxy potatoes
salad leaves
$^1/_2$ cooked chicken, broken into bite-sized chunks
stuffing from the ready-cooked chicken (optional)
3 spring onions, sliced
1 cup crunchy bean sprouts

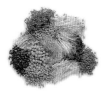

Use a cooked seasoned chicken from the super-market and make this while the chicken is still warm — so easy and just wonderful!

Scrub the potatoes and microwave, steam, boil or bake whole. Slice into thick rings while still warm. Arrange a generous quantity of salad leaves on serving plates. Top with the potato slices, chicken, chicken stuffing, spring onions and sprouts. Blend the sour cream, milk, and chilli mustard together. Spoon over individual portions. Serve immediately. Serves 4.

Dressing

$^1/_2$ cup light sour cream
$^1/_4$ cup milk
1 Tbsp chilli mustard

To keep potatoes at their best take them out of the plastic bag, unless they're in the special green-guard bag. Potatoes like a cool, dark place; a paper bag or cardboard box is perfect.

500 g sausage meat
1 onion, finely chopped
2 medium-sized (500 g) kumara, grated
1 apple, unpeeled and grated
1 cup grated tasty cheese
4 eggs, beaten
$1/4$ tsp ground nutmeg
freshly ground black pepper

Served hot or cold, this slice is terrific family food!

With wet hands, line a 23 cm diameter quiche dish with the sausage meat. Place the onion, kumara, apple, cheese and beaten eggs in a bowl; mix well. Pile into the sausage meat case. Gently press down. Sprinkle with the nutmeg and freshly ground black pepper. Bake at 180˚C for 40-45 minutes until golden brown and set in the middle. Serves 4.

Pumpkin and carrot also work well in this slice. Try them as a change from some or all of the kumara.

Sausage and Kumara Slice

Caramelised Upside-down Tart

2 Tbsp butter
4 cups whole peeled shallots
    OR chunky sliced onions
2 cloves garlic, sliced
2 Tbsp butter
2 Tbsp brown sugar
2 Tbsp vinegar
scone or bread dough (see box)

To peel shallots easily, soak for about 5 minutes in boiled water first.

Dough

I have a bread maker so I use one third of a 4¹/₂-cup flour batch of bread dough and make the rest into bread rolls.

This scone dough is also good, and quicker if you don't have a bread maker.

¹/₃ cup milk
1 egg
2 Tbsp oil
1¹/₂ cups self-raising flour
Beat the milk, egg and oil together. Pour into the flour and mix to form a stiff dough.

If your pan isn't ovenproof, transfer to a quiche dish before adding the dough.

Melt the first measure of butter in a heavy-based ovenproof pan over a gentle heat. Add the shallots and garlic. Cover and simmer over a very low heat for 25-35 minutes or until golden, succulent and moist. Add the second measure of butter, then the brown sugar and vinegar. Cook a further 2-3 minutes until syrupy. Remove from the heat. Roll the dough out to form a circle the same size as the pan. Place on top of the vegetable mix, tucking in around the edges of the pan to seal. If using bread dough, allow it to rise before baking. Bake at 180°C for 12-15 minutes or until golden brown. Leave in pan until ready to serve. Run a knife around the edge of the dish to loosen crust, place a large plate over the tart and tip upside down. Lift off the pan to reveal the glazed shallot topping. Delicious hot or cold. Serves 4-6.

Tomato Fritters

Great with a leafy salad and salsa, this is real family food that both you and your children will love.

1 cup self-raising flour
2 eggs
freshly ground black pepper
2 Tbsp water
2 cups roughly chopped tomatoes
1 Tbsp oil for frying

Place the flour in a bowl and make a well in the centre. Add the eggs, pepper and water. Mix to form a soft dough, add the tomatoes and stir vigorously to achieve a sloppy mix. Heat the oil in a non-stick frying pan. Spoon in portions of the mixture to make fritters. Turn over when the fritters begin to bubble. Cook the other side until golden brown. Place on a paper towel and keep warm. Repeat until all the mixture is used.
Serves 4.

Tomato Salsa

Always choose New Zealand-grown tomatoes. They're ripened on the vine and therefore much sweeter and juicier.

2-3 tomatoes, diced
1 spring onion, finely sliced
freshly ground black pepper
1 Tbsp sweet chilli sauce

You can't get this flavour out of a can — fantastic with barbecued meat, corn chips, cheese and crackers ... or potato wedges!

Mix all ingredients together. Add more chilli sauce if you prefer it hotter.
Makes approximately 1¹/₂ cups.

Kumara Meal in a Moment

Choose one medium-sized kumara per person. Scrub, pierce and microwave on high for 3 minutes each or until soft. Split and add your chosen filling. Serve with salad vegetables — lettuce, sprouts, cucumber, radishes and tomatoes.

Bacon and apple Finely chopped cooked bacon, unpeeled grated apple, light sour cream, chives or parsley.

Pickle 'n' cheese Your favourite pickle, thin slices of cheddar cheese, sour cream.

Mussels Finely chopped mussels, coconut cream, black pepper, finely sliced spring onions.

Mediterranean Chopped ham or salami, roughly chopped tomatoes, pesto sauce, grated parmesan cheese.

Because microwave ovens vary so much, it is difficult to give exact cooking times. If your microwave has one, use the automatic function to take out all the guesswork — perfect!

2 Tbsp oil
4 cups (600 g) diced raw potato and/or
  pumpkin
1 bunch (about 4 cups, 150 g) spinach,
  washed and thick stalks removed
4 eggs
salt and pepper
freshly grated nutmeg (optional)

*If you can make scrambled eggs, you can
make this! When the egg sets, you could
add grated cheese to the top and pop under
the grill until golden and bubbly.*

Heat the oil in a non-stick 24 cm
diameter frying pan, add the potatoes
and pumpkin and cook over a moderate heat for 10 minutes or until
tender. Add the spinach, cover and
cook for another minute or two, just
until the spinach has wilted down.
Beat the eggs and seasonings together,
pour over the potato mixture and cook
without stirring for 5-8 minutes over a
low heat or until the egg has set.
Serve hot in generous wedges, by itself
or with a simple salad.
Serves 4.

Potato and Spinach Tortilla

4–6 waxy potatoes
4 tomatoes, sliced into wedges
100 g feta cheese, cubed
1 small red-skinned onion, cut into rings
3 peppers, roasted
8-10 slices salami, halved
$^1/_2$ cup olives
$^1/_2$ cup finely chopped fresh parsley

Mediterranean-style Potato Salad

*This salad is a great meal by itself!
Use the dressing given, or your
favourite bought one. Add some
pesto sauce to the vinaigrette for
another variation.*

*To roast peppers, halve and
de-seed them. Grill, skin side
up, until the skin blisters and
blackens. Cover with a paper
towel while they cool, then just
slip the skins off.*

Scrub the potatoes and
microwave, steam, boil or bake
whole. Slice into thick wedges
while still warm. Place the
potato, tomatoes, cheese,
onion, peppers, salami, olives
and parsley on serving plates.
Blend the oil, vinegar and
sugar together. Pour over the
salad. Serve hot, warm or cold.
Serves 4

Dressing

*$^1/_4$ cup oil
2 Tbsp red wine vinegar or lemon juice
1 tsp sugar*

4-6 large (600 g) floury potatoes
1-2 tsp paprika
1 tsp mustard powder
$^1/_4$ cup flour
pinch of salt (optional)
$^1/_2$ tsp ground pepper
2 Tbsp oil or clarified butter

Basic Crunchy Wedges

*Experiment with other spices in these basic wedges —
try curry powder, cajun powder, garlic pepper or even a
sprinkling of caraway or mustard seeds.*

Preheat the oven to 200°C. Scrub the potatoes,
but do not peel them. Cut into wedges. Place the
potatoes, paprika, mustard powder, flour, salt and
pepper in a plastic bag. Shake well to evenly coat
the potatoes. Heat the oil in the baking dish for
2-3 minutes before adding the wedges. Bake,
uncovered, at 200°C for 25-35 minutes or until
golden brown and crunchy. Turn once during
cooking. Serve with light sour cream and/or salsa
if desired. See page 26 for a recipe for Tomato
Salsa.
Serves 4.

*Homemade Chicken 'n' Chips,
Fish 'n' Chips or
Sausages 'n' Chips*

Make a batch of Basic Crunchy Wedges and add
either chicken fingers, crumbed fish, calamari
rings or sausages, 15 minutes before the end of
cooking. Children love them and they're cheaper
and healthier than the bought ones!

For each person allow:
1-2 floury potatoes
$^1/_2$ tsp cajun powder
1-2 tomatoes, finely chopped
$^1/_4$ cup grated tasty cheese
$^1/_2$ rasher bacon, finely chopped (optional)
1 Tbsp sour cream

Snack Attack

*Any occasion, any time, this will be a hit!
Bake or boil the potatoes if you don't have
a microwave.*

Microwave the potatoes on high for
3-4 minutes each or until tender.
Slice the potato into wedges and
arrange on an ovenproof plate.
Sprinkle with the cajun powder and
top with the chopped tomato, cheese
and bacon. Grill for 7-10 minutes or
until the cheese is golden brown and
the bacon is cooked and crispy. Top
with the sour cream.

*Always buy potatoes which are
labelled with their variety and
grower. If you know what you
have bought, and you like it,
you can buy it again!*

2 Tbsp oil
2 Tbsp fresh rosemary leaves
6 medium (750 g) potatoes, scrubbed
  and cut into wedges or chunks
8 baby onions, peeled
6 unpeeled cloves of garlic
3 cups chopped seasonal vegetables e.g.
  carrot, parsnip, pumpkin, kumara,
  yams, courgette, scaloppini or pepper
3 rashers lean bacon, cut into strips and
  rolled (optional)
2 (200 g) lean sausages (optional)

A firm favourite in our family.

Mix the oil, rosemary, potatoes, onions,
garlic, seasonal vegetables and bacon in
a roasting dish. Using wet hands,
squeeze small balls of sausage meat out
of the sausage skins and drop into the
pan of vegetables. Bake uncovered in a
hot oven for 45-55 minutes or until the
potatoes are golden and tender. Turn
once during cooking.
Serves 4 as a main meal or 8 as a snack.

*When cooking vegetables, cut
them into pieces of the same
size so they'll cook at the same
speed.*

Chunky Roast Vegetable Medley

Salads

6 medium tomatoes, sliced into wedges
2 cups cucumber chunks
1 cup celery leaves

Tomato and Cucumber Salad

This is a subtly flavoured salad which tastes best when you use the light green leaves from the middle of the celery bunch.

Place the tomatoes, cucumber and celery leaves onto a serving platter. Blend the vinegar, oil, mustard and sugar together. Pour over the salad and toss gently just before serving.
Serves 4.

With all these salads you can use the dressing given, or your favourite bought one.

Dressing

1 Tbsp cider vinegar
1 Tbsp oil
2 tsp whole seed mustard
1 Tbsp brown sugar

4-6 tomatoes, sliced
1-2 red onions, finely sliced into rings
1 cup fresh basil leaves, lightly torn if
   the leaves are large
freshly ground black pepper

*Ample proof that fresh and simple tastes
best!*

Layer the tomatoes, onion and basil
on a serving platter. Place the vinegar,
oil and sugar in a screw-top jar and
shake until the sugar dissolves. Pour
over the salad. Season generously with
the pepper.
Serves 4.

*For really tasty tomatoes, store
them at room temperature out
of direct sunlight, not in the
fridge.*

Dressing

*¹/₄ cup spiced vinegar
2 Tbsp oil
1 tsp sugar*

Super Simple Tomato Salad

Slow-roasted Tomatoes

If you are a fan of sun-dried tomatoes, you will adore these — they have all the taste of sun-dried but none of the tough texture — fantastic! Prepare as many tomatoes as you wish. They may be stored, packed in olive oil for 5-7 days in the refrigerator, but I'd be surprised if you have any left over!

Cut the tomatoes in half and place in a single layer in a roasting pan. Sprinkle with sea salt and freshly ground black pepper and drizzle with a very little olive oil. Bake at 150°C for 1½ hours (or 1 hour in a fan-forced oven). The tomatoes should retain their shape, but be shrivelled, highly coloured and fragrant. Let cool and serve at room temperature.

Ideal to serve whenever you would use sun-dried tomatoes. Try them in fresh rolls as photographed here.

Slow-roasted Tomato Salad

4-5 cups mesclun mix/lettuce leaves
   (include some fresh basil leaves if
   you have them)
6-8 tomatoes, slow-roasted as above
¼ cup black olives (optional)

Dressing

3 Tbsp olive oil
2 Tbsp vinegar or lemon juice
1 tsp sugar
2 Tbsp prepared pesto sauce

Simple elegance, stunning flavour …

Place mesclun, tomatoes and olives on a salad platter. Blend the oil, vinegar, sugar and pesto together. Pour over salad and toss lightly.
Serves 4-5.

2 cups snow peas
3 cups cherry tomatoes
1 packet cress sprouts
freshly ground black pepper

Very easy and great flavour combinations!

Blanch the snow peas in boiling water for 2-3 minutes until bright green and still a little crunchy. Drain and quickly cool under cold running water to prevent further cooking. Scatter with the cherry tomatoes on your serving platter. Snip the cress sprouts and add to the salad in little 'bunches'. Place the shallots, lemon juice, oil and sugar in a screw-top jar and shake vigorously until the sugar is dissolved. Drizzle over the salad and season with the pepper if desired.
Serves 4.

Cherry Tomato Salad

Shallots have a more delicate, sweet taste and finer texture than onions. In this recipe you could substitute spring onions if you don't have shallots — but give them a try — they're delicious!

Dressing

1-2 shallots, finely chopped
1 Tbsp lemon juice
1 Tbsp olive oil
2 tsp sugar

Asparagus and Potato Salad

400 g waxy potatoes, scrubbed
500 g asparagus
4 or 5 small tomatoes, cut into chunky slices

The secret of this salad is to use lovely new-season waxy potatoes! You can use the asparagus raw, especially the purple variety.

Boil the potatoes for 12-15 minutes until just tender. Drain. Cut the asparagus stems into thirds. Cook in boiling water for 3-4 minutes. Cool under cold running water. Mix the lemon juice, oil, sugar, garlic and parsley together. Cut the warm potatoes into halves or quarters. Place the potatoes, asparagus and tomatoes on a serving platter. Pour over the vinaigrette and set aside to cool. Turn gently once or twice. Serves 4.

To keep asparagus spears crisp and fresh treat them like flowers and stand them in a little water in the fridge. Don't keep them for long; asparagus is at its best very fresh.

Dressing

¼ cup lemon juice or cider vinegar
¼ cup olive oil
2 Tbsp sugar
1-2 cloves garlic, finely chopped
2 Tbsp finely chopped fresh parsley

3 cups finely shredded green (smooth or crinkly) cabbage
2 spring onions, sliced
1/4 cup finely chopped fresh mint
3 tomatoes, cut into wedges

Reacquaint yourself with an old favourite — with a flavour twist.

Place the cabbage, onions and mint in a large bowl. Blend the dressing ingredients together. Pour over the salad. Mix thoroughly, lightly toss in the tomato wedges.
Serves 4.

A range of cabbage varieties ensures a year round supply. This salad works well with smooth, crinkly or Asian varieties.

Dressing

2 Tbsp oil
2 Tbsp lemon juice
1/2 tsp ground cumin
1/2 tsp sugar

Crunchy Green Salad

2-3 medium carrots, finely cut or grated
  OR 2 cups baby carrots
2 stalks celery, sliced
Choose 2-4 Tbsp of any of the
  following: walnuts; coconut threads
  or flakes; raisins; toasted sesame,
  sunflower or pumpkin seeds

Carrot and Celery Salad

Classic flavour combinations make this a perennial favourite.

Place the carrot, celery and selected seeds, nuts or raisins in a bowl. Blend the dressing ingredients together. Pour over the salad and toss gently. Garnish with celery leaves.
Serves 4.

Dressing

2 Tbsp oil
2 Tbsp lemon juice
1 tsp sugar
freshly ground black pepper

Notice how even the way you cut your vegetables makes a big difference to the finished dish!

4-5 medium (700 g) kumara
2 bananas, peeled and sliced
¹/₄ cup roughly chopped blanched peanuts
2 spring onions, finely sliced

Kumara and Banana Salad

Use the lemon vinaigrette below or just add a little grated lemon peel to a bought one.

Microwave the kumara on high for 10-12 minutes or until tender. Alternatively, boil or steam for 15-20 minutes. Cut into chunks. Place the kumara, bananas, peanuts and spring onions in a bowl. Blend dressing ingredients together. Pour over the salad and turn gently.
Serves 4-6.

Store kumara in a cool dark place, not in a plastic bag or the fridge. A cardboard box in a cupboard is great.

Dressing

2 Tbsp lemon rind
¹/₄ cup lemon juice
¹/₄ cup oil
1 Tbsp sugar
freshly ground black pepper
¹/₄ cup coriander leaves (optional)

3 cups finely shredded red cabbage
1 medium red onion, finely sliced
$^1/_2$ cup raisins
1 green apple, sliced

Crunchy Red Salad

This salad has a combination of flavours you'll want to make again and again. The dressing can be creamy or vinaigrette-style — your choice.

Place cabbage, onion, raisins and apples in a large bowl. Blend the dressing ingredients together. Pour over the salad and toss if desired.
Serves 4.

Dressing

1 Tbsp oil OR 2 Tbsp light sour cream
1 Tbsp lemon juice
$^1/_2$ tsp prepared horseradish sauce

Salads don't have to be complicated to taste and look great!

Slice a telegraph cucumber lengthwise with either a cheese slicer or a vegetable peeler. Serve either as is, or on a bed of red lettuce with fresh herbs and a sprinkling of balsamic vinegar.

The skin of a telegraph cucumber is very tender so you don't need to peel it. The seeds are also tender so you can eat them too!

Cucumber Salad

Accompaniments

Honeyed Vegetables

6 cups assorted vegetables
(sliced courgettes, leeks, celery,
carrots, asparagus or cabbage,
broccoli or cauliflower florets,
chopped green pepper or bean sprouts)

*Capturing the essence of spring, this is
a great recipe for tempting cautious
vegetable eaters!*

Stir-fry the vegetables over a high heat for 8-10
minutes or until tender but still slightly crisp. Mix all
the honey dressing ingredients together and gently
heat in a saucepan or microwave until the honey
is melted. Pour the hot dressing over the warm
vegetables. Serve immediately.
Serves 4.

Honey Dressing

2 Tbsp honey
2 Tbsp vinegar
1 Tbsp oil
1 Tbsp finely grated fresh ginger

*When stir-frying, heat a little oil and start by
cooking the most dense vegetables, such as carrots or onions, first. Add other vegetables like
cauliflower and broccoli as you cook. Delicate
vegetables, such as snow peas and bean sprouts,
should be added at the last minute.*

2 Tbsp oil
3 medium kumara, scrubbed and cut
into 1 cm slices
2 large carrots, unpeeled, cut into 1 cm
slices
2 cloves garlic, finely sliced
Honey Dressing, see page 54

*A simple and elegant accompaniment.
Note the lower cooking temperature for this
stir-fry.*

Heat the oil in a pan or wok. Add the
kumara, carrot and garlic. Sauté over a
medium heat for 10-12 minutes or
until the kumara is golden brown and
tender. Transfer to a serving dish.
Gently warm the honey dressing
ingredients and pour over the
vegetables. Sprinkle with fresh
coriander leaves if desired.
Serves 4.

*If your stir-fry starts to dry out,
add a little water. The steam
will add moisture and help to
cook the vegetables.*

Succulent Root Vegetables

1 Tbsp oil
2 onions, sliced into wedges
2-3 stalks of celery, cut into
   chunky diagonal slices
1/2 tsp Chinese five spice powder
4 cups prepared Chinese cabbage
   (use the leaves whole, and prepare for
   cooking by simply washing, then cutting off the thick base of the stalks)

Asian Vegetables

Heat the oil in a large frying
pan or wok. Add the onions
and celery, cook for 2-3
minutes. If the pan dries out,
add a little water. Add the bok
choy and the five spice.
Stir-fry over a high heat for 2-3
minutes, stirring continuously.
Serve immediately.
Serves 4.

There are many different types of Chinese cabbage available. In general they are all suitable for quick cooking methods such as stir-frying. The names of these cabbages can be quite confusing as they often have different names in different areas of China. For this recipe use either Chinese white cabbage (baak choi, bak choy, bok choy, pak choy), flowering Chinese cabbage (choi sum) or Peking cabbage (wong nga baak).

For a great lunch or snack in less than five minutes, spread fresh bread with sour cream and whole seed mustard. Cook fresh asparagus (see instructions below), drain, roll up in the bread while still warm.

Real Asparagus Rolls

To cook asparagus

Boiling
Use a large pan and lay the whole or cut spears in sufficient boiling water to cover them. Simmer for 5-8 minutes or until tender but still slightly crisp.

Microwave
Place 300 g asparagus in a flat dish. Add ¼ cup of water. Cover and cook on high for 3-5 minutes or until tender. Pieces will cook more quickly than whole spears.

Stir-fry
Cut into bite-sized chunks and sauté in a little hot oil for 3-4 minutes.

2 Tbsp oil
2 bunches asparagus, cut into generous
   bite-sized lengths
4-5 small courgettes, in chunky slices
1 cup adzuki or crunchy combo sprouts

The sprouts in this wonderfully easy stir-fry give it a lovely nutty flavour and texture!

Heat the oil in a non-stick pan or wok. Sauté the asparagus and courgettes for 3-4 minutes or until barely tender. Toss in the sprouts just before serving.
Serves 4.

Asparagus Stir-fry

6 medium waxy potatoes
$^{1}/_{2}$ cucumber
4 tomatoes
1 avocado
1 tsp caraway seeds

Potatoes with Avocado

Scrub the potatoes and microwave, steam, boil or bake whole. Cut the potatoes, cucumber, tomatoes and avocado into bite-sized chunks. Place in a serving bowl. Using a food processor make the dressing by blending the onion, garlic, sugar, vinegar, oil and water together until thick and creamy. Pour the dressing over the potatoes, sprinkle with the caraway seeds and mix well.
Serves 4-5.

Dressing

If you don't have a food processor to make the dressing, just chop the onion and garlic very finely and mix with the remaining ingredients. This dressing is fantastic with any potato- or kumara-based salad.

1 small onion, peeled	*2 Tbsp vinegar*
1 clove garlic, peeled	*2 Tbsp oil*
2 Tbsp sugar	*2 Tbsp water*

Instant Tomato Sauce

4 (300 g) fully ripe tomatoes
¹/4 cup fresh basil, coriander or parsley
freshly ground black pepper

A fresh, tasty, versatile sauce. Serve over any cooked meat, fish, chicken, pasta, pizza or vegetables like potatoes, broccoli or beans.

Place all ingredients in a food processor and process until smooth. This sauce will keep for two days refrigerated. It will separate on standing; simply stir well before serving.
Makes 1¹/2 cups.

Grilled Tomatoes

4 medium tomatoes
finely chopped fresh basil,
   thyme or rosemary
freshly ground black pepper

Great for breakfast, lunch or dinner!

Halve the tomatoes and place cut side up in a baking dish. Sprinkle with the herbs and pepper. Bake in a moderate oven until the tomatoes are tender or grill for 10-12 minutes.

Tin Foil Parcels

Vegetables cooked this way are easy, succulent and full of flavour. Some of my favourites are onion rings with fresh rosemary or sage, peppers with shallots, beans (or asparagus) with sesame seeds, corn on the cob, and courgettes with garlic.

Cut the vegetables into pieces the same size (leave corn on the cob whole). Place the prepared vegetables on a large piece of tin foil. Add a sprinkling of oil or 1 or 2 dabs of butter. Season generously with freshly ground black pepper. Fold up to form a secure, watertight parcel. Barbecue for about the same time as you would stir-fry that vegetable, turning over several times during cooking.

Most stir-fry recipes taste delicious when barbecued in a tin foil parcel.

3-4 medium (600 g) kumara, sliced
  thinly (¹/₂ cm thick)
1-2 red or green peppers, cut into
  chunky wedges
¹/₄ cup lemon juice
2 Tbsp oil
2 Tbsp runny honey
lettuce leaves to serve (optional)

*Roast kumara is everyone's favourite. These
delicious honey-roasted kumara are perfect
straight from the oven, or cooled to serve as
a salad.*

Place the vegetables in a roasting pan.
Combine the lemon juice, oil and
honey. Pour over the vegetables and
marinate if possible. Bake at 200°C for
20-25 minutes or until tender and
golden brown. Serve immediately, or
cool slightly and toss through lettuce
leaves.
Serves 4-6.

*Use a mixture of red, gold and
orange kumara for a great
effect.*

Marinated Roast Kumara

Barbecue Vegetable Platter

Recently developed varieties of eggplant are not bitter and it isn't usually necessary to salt and soak the slices before cooking as some older recipe books may instruct.

Traditionally we serve salads with barbecues, but cooked vegetables make a delightful change. Try making a barbecued vegetable platter with some or all of the following. Add extra flavourings if you want — garlic, root ginger or chilli are wonderful!

Onion wedges or rings

Peel and cut the onions into wedges or rings. Brush sparingly with oil. Using a solid barbecue plate stir-fry for 6-8 minutes or until golden and softened.

Tomato halves
Cut the tomatoes in half and place face down on the barbecue plate. Cook for about 3-4 minutes or until heated through. Turn over and sprinkle with pepper or fresh herbs. Remove from heat and serve immediately.

Pepper strips Cut the pepper lengthways into quarters or eighths. Remove the seeds. Place on a hot barbecue plate, brush sparingly with oil and cook for 5–6 minutes, turning frequently during cooking.

Courgette halves Split the courgettes in half lengthways and place on the barbecue. Baste sparingly with oil and cook for 5–6 minutes, turning frequently during cooking.

Potatoes Partly cook the potatoes in the microwave. Cut into wedges and brush with oil. Cook about 8-10 minutes on a solid barbecue plate.

OR scrub medium-sized floury potatoes, but do not peel them. Wrap in a double layer of foil and place in barbecue embers. Check after 25-30 minutes.

Kumara Cook whole as for potatoes (above) or cut into $\frac{1}{2}$ cm slices, brush with oil and turn only once or twice during cooking. They will take 10-12 minutes.

Eggplant slices are fantastic. Brush generously with oil as they cook. They'll take about 5-10 minutes.

Other vegetables like fresh asparagus, snow peas, baby corn, yams, scaloppini, etc. are all delicious. Some only require a brief cooking time, depending on how vicious your barbecue is!

Barbecue Medley

2 medium peppers, de-seeded and cut
into chunky wedges
3 courgettes
OR 1 medium eggplant, in 1 cm slices
or slabs
2 onions, cut into wedges
8-10 whole unpeeled cloves of garlic
2 medium kumara, peeled and sliced into
$^1/_2$ cm slabs
$^1/_4$ cup olive oil
2 cloves garlic, crushed
1 Tbsp brown sugar
freshly ground black pepper

*This is a great addition to barbecue food! It can
also be baked, grilled or even stir-fried in a wok
or large pan. Cut the vegetables into big bold
pieces for easy cooking and the best effect.*

Place all the prepared vegetables in a
baking dish. Combine the oil, crushed
garlic, sugar and pepper. Stir into the
vegetables to coat evenly. Cook on a
medium to hot barbecue plate for about
10 minutes or until tender.
Serves 4-6.

*When cutting onions into
wedges for this dish, leave the
root end on, that way the
onion wedges stay intact as
they cook.*

Perfect Roast Vegetables

Preheat the oven to 200°C. Cut the vegetables into chunks (potatoes, pumpkin, kumara, carrots, parsnips and onions), or leave whole (yams, shallots, baby beetroot). You only have to peel the onions. Make sure they are reasonably dry and add 1-2 Tbsp oil or clarified butter. Most roast vegetables take about an hour to cook — if they are all about egg-sized. Reduce the size of the pieces if you are in a hurry.

Roast vegetables with a difference ... Try cutting the vegetables differently, or adding a light sprinkling of seasonings. There are so many tempting flavours to try. Here are some suggestions.

Potato Hedgehogs Place a wooden spoon on one side of a scrubbed potato, so you can't cut right through, then cut into small squares. Brush with oil and sprinkle with parmesan cheese. See top of photograph, page 69.

Criss-cross Potatoes Halve a
potato, or kumara, and cut criss-cross
patterns with a sharp knife. Or surprise
the kids — with a face or their initials!
Brush with oil. Add raisin 'eyes' after
cooking. See middle and bottom of
photograph, right.

Parsnip Cut into thick diagonal
slices and sprinkle with Italian herb mix.
(See photograph page 68)

**Onion quarters and potato
chunks** Sprinkle with cajun spice
mix.

Pumpkin and kumara
Sprinkle with ground ginger and
coriander.

'Soft' vegetables such as
capsicum, asparagus, courgette and
tomatoes are great roasted. Cut into
large chunks, oil lightly and bake until
tender— 15-20 minutes.

*Roast vegetables in a separate
pan from your meat and they
won't soak up the fat — much
tastier and healthier.*

Index